50 Kyoto Palette Recipes

By: Kelly Johnson

Table of Contents

- Yudofu (Hot Tofu)
- Kaiseki Bento
- Nishin Soba (Herring Soba)
- Yuba Donburi (Tofu Skin Rice Bowl)
- Kyo Tsukemono (Kyoto Pickles)
- Obanzai Vegetable Stir-Fry
- Kyo-Tamago (Kyoto-style Egg Omelet)
- Kabocha Nimono (Simmered Pumpkin)
- Matcha Tofu Cheesecake
- Goma Dofu (Sesame Tofu)
- Shojin Ryori Soup
- Kyoto Miso Nasu (Miso Eggplant)
- Nama-Fu Dengaku (Grilled Wheat Gluten)
- Satsuma Imo Rice
- Takenoko Gohan (Bamboo Shoot Rice)
- Dashimaki Tamago
- Kinpira Gobo (Burdock Root Stir-Fry)

- Yatsuhashi (Cinnamon Rice Sweets)
- Agedashi Yuba
- Komatsuna Ohitashi (Blanched Mustard Greens)
- Grilled Ayu with Salt
- Matcha Warabi Mochi
- Kyoto-style Zoni (New Year's Soup)
- Tofu Karaage
- Kyo-Baigan (Kyoto Eggplant) Grill
- Sansai Soba (Mountain Vegetable Soba)
- Yuba Salad with Ponzu
- Somen Noodles with Yuzu
- Kuri Gohan (Chestnut Rice)
- Miso Dengaku Skewers
- Chawanmushi with Ginkgo Nuts
- Kyoto Gohan Roll
- Nanzenji-style Vegetable Medley
- Matcha Ice Cream with Red Beans
- Soy Milk Nabe
- Yuba and Daikon Simmer

- Kyoto Sweet Potato Croquettes

- Matcha Mont Blanc

- Hijiki Seaweed Nimono

- Kinako Mochi

- Chrysanthemum Leaf Salad

- Kyo-style Vegetable Tempura

- Dashi-marinated Tomatoes

- Simmered Lotus Root with Yuzu

- Hojicha Jelly

- Azuki Red Bean Rice

- Myoga Pickle with Ginger

- Kyoto Plum Vinegar Pickles

- Grilled Kyoto-style Tofu

- Matcha Chiffon Cake

Yudofu (Hot Tofu)

Ingredients:

- 1 block silken or soft tofu
- Kombu (dried kelp)
- Water

For dipping sauce:

- Soy sauce
- Grated ginger
- Chopped scallions
- Bonito flakes (optional)

Instructions:

1. Place kombu in a pot of water and let it soak for 20 minutes.
2. Slowly heat the water with kombu. Just before boiling, remove kombu.
3. Gently add tofu and heat through without breaking it (5–7 minutes).
4. Serve with dipping sauce and toppings on the side.

Kaiseki Bento (Traditional Kyoto Lunch Box)

(Note: A combination of several small seasonal dishes)
Common items:

- Grilled fish (e.g., miso-marinated salmon)
- Pickled vegetables
- Tamagoyaki
- Simmered vegetables (like kabocha or lotus root)
- Rice with black sesame
- A seasonal fruit or wagashi sweet

Assembly Tip:
Neatly arrange in separate compartments. Emphasize seasonality and color harmony.

Nishin Soba (Herring Soba Noodles)

Ingredients:

- Dried herring (simmered in soy/sugar mix) or pre-cooked nishin
- Soba noodles
- Dashi broth
- Soy sauce, mirin, sugar

Instructions:

1. Simmer herring in soy sauce, mirin, and sugar until sweet and tender.
2. Cook soba noodles, rinse, and set aside.
3. Prepare broth: mix dashi, soy sauce, mirin. Heat through.
4. Place noodles in a bowl, pour broth, and top with simmered herring.

Yuba Donburi (Tofu Skin Rice Bowl)

Ingredients:

- Fresh yuba (tofu skin)
- Cooked rice
- Soy sauce, mirin, dashi for simmering
- Optional: wasabi or grated ginger

Instructions:

1. Simmer yuba in soy-mirin-dashi mix until warmed and flavored.
2. Serve over rice with broth and a touch of wasabi or ginger on top.

Kyo Tsukemono (Kyoto Pickles)

Ingredients:

- Daikon, turnip, or cucumber
- Salt
- Rice vinegar
- Sugar
- Kombu and chili pepper (optional)

Instructions:

1. Slice vegetables thinly and sprinkle with salt. Let sit 1–2 hours.
2. Rinse and drain.
3. Mix vinegar, sugar, kombu, and chili. Soak veggies for at least 1 day.

Obanzai Vegetable Stir-Fry

Ingredients:

- Seasonal Kyoto vegetables (eggplant, burdock, shishito peppers, etc.)
- Soy sauce
- Sesame oil
- Mirin
- Optional: katsuobushi or sesame seeds

Instructions:

1. Heat sesame oil in a pan, stir-fry vegetables until tender.
2. Add soy sauce and mirin, cook until slightly caramelized.
3. Top with sesame seeds or bonito flakes.

Kyo-Tamago (Kyoto-style Egg Omelet)

Ingredients:

- 3 eggs
- 1 tbsp dashi
- 1 tsp sugar
- 1/2 tsp soy sauce

Instructions:

1. Beat all ingredients until smooth.
2. Cook in layers in a square tamagoyaki pan, rolling each layer.
3. Slice into neat squares and serve warm or chilled.

Kabocha Nimono (Simmered Pumpkin)

Ingredients:

- 1/4 kabocha, cut into chunks
- Dashi, soy sauce, mirin, sugar

Instructions:

1. Simmer kabocha in dashi, soy sauce, mirin, and sugar until tender.
2. Let cool slightly in the broth to absorb more flavor.

Matcha Tofu Cheesecake

Ingredients:

- 1 block silken tofu
- 200g cream cheese
- 1/3 cup sugar
- 2 tbsp matcha powder
- 1 egg
- Cookie crust (optional)

Instructions:

1. Blend tofu, cream cheese, sugar, matcha, and egg until smooth.
2. Pour into a lined pan or crust and bake at 325°F (160°C) for 35–40 min.
3. Cool and chill before slicing.

Goma Dofu (Sesame Tofu)

Ingredients:

- 1/2 cup sesame paste
- 2 tbsp kudzu starch (or cornstarch)
- 1 1/4 cups water

Instructions:

1. Dissolve kudzu in water, then mix in sesame paste.
2. Stir constantly over medium heat until thick and glossy.
3. Pour into a mold and chill until firm.
4. Serve with soy sauce or wasabi.

Shojin Ryori Soup (Zen Buddhist Vegetable Soup)

Ingredients:

- Kombu dashi
- Shiitake mushrooms
- Carrot
- Daikon
- Snow peas or spinach
- Soy sauce
- Mirin

Instructions:

1. Prepare kombu dashi and bring to a simmer.
2. Slice all vegetables evenly and add to the dashi.
3. Simmer until just tender.
4. Season with soy sauce and a dash of mirin.
5. Serve warm, garnished with snow peas.

Kyoto Miso Nasu (Grilled Miso Eggplant)

Ingredients:

- Japanese eggplant (nasu)
- Miso paste
- Mirin
- Sugar
- Sake

Instructions:

1. Slice eggplants lengthwise and grill or pan-sear until soft.
2. Mix miso, mirin, sugar, and sake into a thick glaze.
3. Spread glaze on eggplant and broil until golden.

Nama-Fu Dengaku (Grilled Wheat Gluten Skewers)

Ingredients:

- Nama-fu (fresh wheat gluten, often colored/marbled)
- Miso, sugar, mirin, and sake for dengaku miso sauce
- Bamboo skewers

Instructions:

1. Slice nama-fu and skewer.
2. Grill lightly until crisp outside.
3. Brush with sweet miso glaze and grill again briefly.

Satsuma Imo Gohan (Sweet Potato Rice)

Ingredients:

- Japanese sweet potato (satsuma imo), cubed
- Japanese short-grain rice
- Salt
- Optional: black sesame seeds

Instructions:

1. Wash and soak rice, then drain.
2. Mix rice, sweet potato cubes, water, and a pinch of salt.
3. Cook as usual in rice cooker or pot.
4. Sprinkle black sesame seeds on top before serving.

Takenoko Gohan (Bamboo Shoot Rice)

Ingredients:

- Boiled bamboo shoots, sliced
- Short-grain rice
- Kombu
- Soy sauce, mirin, sake

Instructions:

1. Wash and soak rice.
2. Add rice, sliced bamboo shoots, kombu, soy sauce, mirin, and sake to rice cooker.
3. Cook and fluff before serving.

Dashimaki Tamago (Dashi-Rolled Omelet)

Ingredients:

- Eggs
- Dashi
- Mirin
- Soy sauce

Instructions:

1. Mix eggs with dashi, soy sauce, and mirin.
2. Cook in a rectangular tamagoyaki pan, rolling in layers.
3. Let cool and slice. Serve warm or chilled.

Kinpira Gobo (Sautéed Burdock Root and Carrot)

Ingredients:

- Burdock root (gobo)
- Carrot
- Soy sauce
- Mirin
- Sesame oil
- Sesame seeds

Instructions:

1. Julienne burdock and carrot. Soak burdock briefly in water.
2. Stir-fry in sesame oil.
3. Add mirin and soy sauce. Cook until slightly caramelized.
4. Sprinkle with sesame seeds.

Yatsuhashi (Cinnamon Rice Sweets)

Ingredients:

- Glutinous rice flour
- Sugar
- Water
- Cinnamon
- Optional: red bean paste

Instructions:

1. Mix rice flour, sugar, water, and cinnamon into a dough.
2. Steam until translucent and sticky.
3. Roll flat and cut into triangles.
4. Optional: fill with anko before folding.

Agedashi Yuba (Fried Tofu Skin in Broth)

Ingredients:

- Fresh yuba
- Potato starch or cornstarch
- Dashi broth
- Soy sauce, mirin
- Grated daikon, scallions

Instructions:

1. Cut yuba into bite-sized pieces and lightly coat in starch.
2. Deep-fry until crispy and golden.
3. Serve in hot dashi-soy-mirin broth.
4. Top with daikon and scallions.

Komatsuna Ohitashi (Blanched Mustard Greens with Dashi Soy Dressing)

Ingredients:

- Komatsuna (Japanese mustard greens) or spinach
- Dashi
- Soy sauce
- Mirin
- Bonito flakes (optional)

Instructions:

1. Blanch komatsuna quickly and chill in ice water.
2. Squeeze out excess water and cut into bite-size pieces.
3. Combine dashi, soy sauce, and mirin for the dressing.
4. Pour over greens and garnish with bonito flakes.

Grilled Ayu (Sweetfish) with Salt

Ingredients:

- Whole ayu (cleaned)
- Sea salt
- Bamboo skewers

Instructions:

1. Skewer fish in a curved "swimming" shape.
2. Lightly salt the skin.
3. Grill slowly over charcoal until crispy outside and tender inside.
4. Serve with lemon or sudachi.

Matcha Warabi Mochi

Ingredients:

- Warabi starch (or substitute with potato starch)
- Sugar
- Water
- Matcha powder
- Kinako (roasted soybean flour)

Instructions:

1. Mix starch, sugar, water, and matcha.
2. Cook over low heat, stirring until thick and translucent.
3. Chill, cut into cubes, and coat with kinako or more matcha.

Kyoto-style Zoni (New Year's Mochi Soup)

Ingredients:

- White miso paste
- Dashi
- Mochi
- Carrot, daikon, and yuba
- Komatsuna or other leafy greens

Instructions:

1. Simmer dashi with sliced daikon and carrot.
2. Dissolve white miso gently into the broth.
3. Add mochi and yuba, simmer until soft.
4. Garnish with greens just before serving.

Tofu Karaage (Crispy Fried Tofu Bites)

Ingredients:

- Firm tofu
- Soy sauce
- Mirin
- Garlic and ginger
- Potato starch for coating
- Oil for frying

Instructions:

1. Press tofu to remove water, then marinate in soy, mirin, garlic, and ginger.
2. Coat with potato starch and fry until golden.
3. Serve with lemon and optional dipping sauce.

Kyo-Baigan Grill (Kyoto Eggplant with Sweet Miso Glaze)

Ingredients:

- Small Kyoto eggplants or Japanese eggplants
- White miso
- Sugar
- Mirin
- Sake

Instructions:

1. Halve and grill eggplants until soft.
2. Mix miso glaze and spread on top.
3. Broil for a few minutes until bubbly and golden.

Sansai Soba (Mountain Vegetable Buckwheat Noodles)

Ingredients:

- Soba noodles
- Assorted sansai (bracken fern, bamboo shoots, fiddleheads)
- Dashi broth
- Soy sauce and mirin

Instructions:

1. Cook soba noodles and rinse in cold water.
2. Heat dashi, soy, and mirin to make soup.
3. Add vegetables to the broth briefly, then pour over soba.
4. Garnish with green onions or yuzu zest.

Yuba Salad with Ponzu Dressing

Ingredients:

- Fresh yuba (tofu skin)
- Mixed greens or mizuna
- Cherry tomatoes
- Cucumber
- Ponzu sauce

Instructions:

1. Tear yuba into strips.
2. Toss greens, tomatoes, cucumber, and yuba.
3. Drizzle with ponzu before serving.

Somen Noodles with Yuzu

Ingredients:

- Somen noodles
- Yuzu zest or juice
- Light dashi dipping sauce
- Green onions and grated ginger

Instructions:

1. Boil somen and cool in ice water.
2. Serve with dipping sauce flavored with yuzu zest.
3. Offer condiments on the side.

Kuri Gohan (Chestnut Rice)

Ingredients:

- Japanese short-grain rice
- Fresh or frozen chestnuts (peeled)
- Salt, mirin, and a touch of soy sauce
- Kombu

Instructions:

1. Soak rice and kombu together for 30 mins.
2. Add chestnuts, salt, soy sauce, and mirin.
3. Cook in rice cooker or donabe.
4. Fluff gently and serve with sesame seeds or a sprinkle of salt.

Miso Dengaku Skewers

Ingredients:

- Firm tofu or eggplant
- White miso
- Sugar, sake, mirin
- Sesame seeds

Instructions:

1. Grill or broil tofu/eggplant.
2. Mix and simmer miso glaze.
3. Skewer ingredients and brush with glaze.
4. Sprinkle with sesame seeds before serving.

Chawanmushi with Ginkgo Nuts

Ingredients:

- Eggs
- Dashi
- Soy sauce, mirin
- Ginkgo nuts, shrimp, kamaboko, mushrooms

Instructions:

1. Mix dashi, soy, and mirin into beaten eggs.
2. Pour into cups with fillings.
3. Steam gently until just set.
4. Garnish with mitsuba or yuzu zest.

Kyoto Gohan Roll

(Think sushi roll meets kaiseki plate)

Ingredients:

- Seasoned rice
- Shiso, cooked veggies (burdock, lotus root), pickles
- Nori or yuba wrap

Instructions:

1. Spread seasoned rice over wrap.
2. Layer vegetables, roll gently.
3. Slice into elegant spirals, serve with ponzu or matcha salt.

Nanzenji-style Vegetable Medley

Ingredients:

- Lotus root, carrot, shiitake, daikon, snow peas
- Light soy-based dashi broth

Instructions:

1. Simmer each veggie type in dashi until just tender.
2. Arrange in seasonal shape or layered in a lacquer box.
3. Serve warm or room temp with yuzu zest or grated ginger.

Matcha Ice Cream with Red Beans

Ingredients:

- High-quality matcha powder
- Heavy cream, milk, sugar
- Cooked sweet red beans (anko)

Instructions:

1. Make matcha custard base and churn into ice cream.
2. Serve scoops topped with warm or chilled anko.
3. Garnish with mochi or kinako if desired.

Soy Milk Nabe

Ingredients:

- Unflavored soy milk
- Dashi
- Napa cabbage, mushrooms, tofu, carrots, udon
- Sesame sauce for dipping

Instructions:

1. Simmer dashi and soy milk gently.
2. Add vegetables and tofu.
3. Let guests cook at table hot pot style.
4. Dip into sesame or ponzu sauces.

Yuba and Daikon Simmer

Ingredients:

- Fresh or dried yuba
- Daikon radish, sliced into rounds
- Dashi, soy, mirin

Instructions:

1. Simmer daikon until soft.
2. Add yuba and simmer with light seasoning.
3. Serve in small bowls with hot broth and grated ginger.

Kyoto Sweet Potato Croquettes

Ingredients:

- Kintoki or satsumaimo sweet potatoes
- Butter, sugar, cream (optional cinnamon)
- Flour, egg, panko

Instructions:

1. Mash sweet potato with butter/sugar.
2. Shape, coat in flour, egg, panko.
3. Deep-fry until golden.
4. Serve hot with kuromitsu drizzle or as-is.

Matcha Mont Blanc

Ingredients:

- Chestnut purée
- Whipped cream
- Matcha powder
- Butter cookie base or sponge cake

Instructions:

1. Whip chestnut purée with cream until smooth.
2. Layer over a crisp base or sponge using a piping bag.
3. Dust with matcha powder and chill.
4. Optionally top with candied chestnut.

Hijiki Seaweed Nimono

Ingredients:

- Dried hijiki
- Carrot, aburaage (fried tofu), soybeans
- Soy sauce, mirin, sugar, dashi

Instructions:

1. Rehydrate hijiki and drain.
2. Stir-fry with vegetables, then simmer in dashi seasoning.
3. Serve chilled or room temp, great as a side.

Kinako Mochi

Ingredients:

- Mochi (store-bought or freshly made)
- Kinako (roasted soybean flour)
- Sugar, a pinch of salt

Instructions:

1. Warm or toast mochi until puffed.
2. Roll in kinako mixed with sugar and a pinch of salt.
3. Serve with kuromitsu syrup if desired.

Chrysanthemum Leaf Salad (Shungiku Salad)

Ingredients:

- Fresh chrysanthemum greens
- Ponzu or sesame dressing
- Toasted sesame seeds, bonito flakes (optional)

Instructions:

1. Blanch greens quickly, then shock in ice water.
2. Drain well, plate with dressing.
3. Garnish with sesame and katsuobushi.

Kyo-style Vegetable Tempura

Ingredients:

- Shiso, sweet potato, eggplant, green beans, kabocha
- Tempura batter (ice cold)
- Dipping tentsuyu sauce or matcha salt

Instructions:

1. Slice vegetables thinly.
2. Coat in light batter and fry quickly.
3. Drain and serve with tentsuyu or flavored salts.

Dashi-marinated Tomatoes

Ingredients:

- Cherry tomatoes (peeled)
- Light dashi broth
- Soy sauce, mirin, sugar

Instructions:

1. Peel tomatoes by blanching briefly.
2. Soak in chilled dashi mixture for several hours.
3. Serve in a small bowl garnished with a mint leaf or shiso.

Simmered Lotus Root with Yuzu

Ingredients:

- Sliced lotus root
- Soy sauce, mirin, dashi
- Fresh yuzu zest or juice

Instructions:

1. Simmer lotus root until tender in dashi blend.
2. Finish with a dash of yuzu juice and zest.
3. Serve warm or chilled with sesame seeds.

Hōjicha Jelly

Ingredients:

- Hōjicha tea (roasted green tea)
- Gelatin or agar
- Honey or kuromitsu syrup

Instructions:

1. Brew strong hōjicha and sweeten to taste.
2. Dissolve gelatin/agar and mix into tea.
3. Chill until firm. Serve in cubes or cups with a drizzle of syrup.

Azuki Red Bean Rice (Sekihan Style)

Ingredients:

- Mochigome (glutinous rice)
- Azuki beans
- Salt, sesame seeds

Instructions:

1. Boil azuki until tender. Reserve the liquid.
2. Steam rice with azuki water, then add beans.
3. Mix gently and top with sesame-salt mix before serving.

Myōga Pickle with Ginger

Ingredients:

- Fresh myōga buds
- Ginger slices
- Rice vinegar, sugar, salt

Instructions:

1. Thinly slice myōga and ginger.
2. Pickle in a sweet vinegar mix for at least 2 hours.
3. Serve chilled as a crisp palate cleanser.

Kyoto Plum Vinegar Pickles (Ume-su-zuke)

Ingredients:

- Seasonal vegetables (daikon, cucumber, turnip)
- Ume plum vinegar
- Sugar, kombu

Instructions:

1. Slice veggies and soak in a mixture of ume vinegar and sugar.
2. Add kombu strips for umami depth.
3. Chill and enjoy with rice or as a garnish.

Grilled Kyoto-style Tofu (Yaki-Dōfu)

Ingredients:

- Firm tofu (pressed and dried)
- Miso or soy sauce glaze
- Green onions or sesame seeds

Instructions:

1. Grill tofu until golden on both sides.
2. Brush with glaze while grilling.
3. Top with green onion or sesame before serving.

Matcha Chiffon Cake

Ingredients:

- Cake flour, sugar
- Eggs, matcha powder
- Vegetable oil, cream of tartar

Instructions:

1. Separate eggs, whip whites to soft peaks.
2. Fold matcha batter with whites gently.
3. Bake in a chiffon mold.
4. Cool upside down and serve with whipped cream or sweet bean paste.